CHILDREN'S ENCYCLOPEDIA
THE WORLD OF KNOWLEDGE

THE EARTH

Manasvi Vohra

V&S PUBLISHERS

Published by:

V&S PUBLISHERS

F-2/16, Ansari road, Daryaganj, New Delhi-110002
☎ 23240026, 23240027 • *Fax:* 011-23240028
Email: info@vspublishers.com • *Website:* www.vspublishers.com

Regional Office : Hyderabad
5-1-707/1, Brij Bhawan (Beside Central Bank of India Lane)
Bank Street, Koti, Hyderabad - 500 095
☎ 040-24737290
E-mail: vspublishershyd@gmail.com

Branch Office : Mumbai
Jaywant Industrial Estate, 2nd Floor-222, Tardeo Road
Opposite Sobo Central, Mumbai - 400 034
☎ 022-23510736
E-mail: vspublishersmum@gmail.com

Follow us on:

All books available at **www.vspublishers.com**

© **Copyright:** V&S PUBLISHERS
Edition 2017

PUBLISHER'S NOTE

V&S Publishers is glad to announce the launch of a unique, set of 12 books under the head, *Children's Encyclopedia – The World of Knowledge.* The set of 12 books namely – *Physices, Chemistry, Space Science, General Sceince, Life Science, Human Body, Electronics & Communications, Scientists, Inventions & Discoveries, Transportation, The Earth, and GK (General Knowledge)* has been especially developed keeping in mind the students and children of all age groups, particularly from 6 to 14 years of age. Our main aim is to arouse the interest and solve the queries of the school children regarding the various and diverse topics of Science and help them master the subject thoroughly.

In the book, *The Earth,* the author focusses on The Earth, All about Earthquakes and Volcanones, Mountains, Oceans, Weather, etc.

Each chapter is followed by a section called **Quick Facts** that contains a set of interesting and fascinating facts about the topics already discussed in the chapter. At the end of the book a **Glossary** of difficult words and scientific terms to make the book complete and comprehensive is given.

Quick Facts

- We can see about 2,000 stars in the sky on a clear, dark night.

Though our aim is to be flawless, but errors might have crept in inadvertently. So we request our esteemed readers to read the book thoroughly and offer valuable suggestions wherever necessary to improve and enhance the quality of the book. Hope it interests you all and serves its purpose well.

CONTENTS

The Earth

THE EARTH

Chapter - 1

THE PLANET, EARTH

The Earth was created about 4.5 billion years ago. It is made of a mass of rocky debris, rich in iron, which was orbiting the Sun. The rocks smashed into the young planet as meteorites, and were welded together by the heat generated from the energy of impact. This impact generated so much heat that the earth completely melted. Then the heavy iron sank towards the centre and became the core of the earth. The lighter rocks, on the other hand, became the **mantle** and the **crust**.

Earth's Structure

The earth's structure resembles that of a *peach*.

- 🍒 The centre of the earth is made up of *iron*. This metallic core resembles the hard stone which is at the centre of the peach.

- 🍒 Then comes the hot, mobile rock of the mantle, which is just like the juicy flesh of the peach.

- 🍒 Then at top is the earth's rocky crust, which is like the skin of the peach.

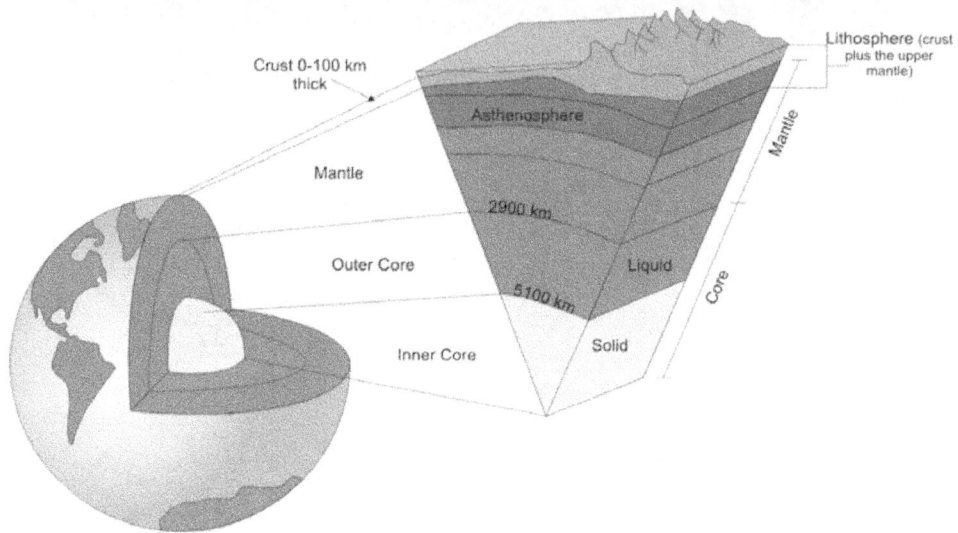

Crust 0-100 km thick
Lithosphere (crust plus the upper mantle)
Asthenosphere
Mantle
2900 km
Outer Core
Liquid
5100 km
Inner Core
Solid
Mantle
Core

Inner Core

The earth's inner core is a heavy ball made up of solid nickel and iron. Nuclear reactions within the earth heat it to about 4,700°C (8,500°F), but it does not melt due to the intense pressure at the core.

Outer Core

A fluid mass of molten sulphur, nickel and iron surrounds the solid inner core of the earth.

Lower Mantle

About 2,900 kilometres (1,800 miles) deep, the rocky mantle is heated to a temperature of about 3,500°C (6,300°F) at its base. Though it does not melt due to the intense pressure, the hot rock continues to move slowly due to the rising heat.

Upper Mantle

The upper mantle is heated to almost 1,000°C (1,800°F). Wherever movement in the mantle causes the cool and brittle crust to crack, reduced pressure makes the hot mantle rock melt and erupt from the volcanoes.

Oceanic Crust

Oceanic crust, which lies between the continents, is less than 11 kilometres (7 miles) thick. Made of heavy rocks that erupt from the hot mantle at mid-ocean ridges, it forms the bedrock of the ocean floors.

Continental Crust

The lightest rocks of the earth combine and form *large slabs*. They float on the mantle, which is quite heavy. Nearly 70 kilometres (45 miles) thick, they rise above the sea level and form the continents we live on.

Land Surface

Sunlight, rain, wind, frost, etc., breakdown the rocks on land. This exposure to erosion (process of removal of the earth's top layer) and weathering (*breakdown* of rocks, minerals and soils as a result of contact with the earth's atmosphere) releases minerals which are essential for the survival of various plants and other life forms.

Oceans

The areas lying between the continents are filled with *large masses of water called the oceans*. Most of the water erupted from volcanoes as water vapour early in the earth's history. They caused torrential rains which resulted in the formation of rivers, seas and oceans. Even the melting of ice resulted in the formation of oceans.

Weather Systems

Due to the sun's heat, the water vapour from the oceans rise into the lower atmosphere. This water gets collected and forms large masses of clouds. The clouds then spill rain onto the continents, allowing life to exist on land.

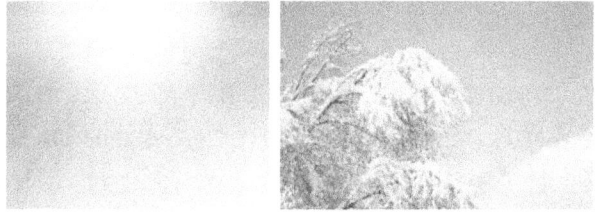

Atmosphere

The earth's atmosphere is made up of many gases including *oxygen, carbon dioxide* and *nitrogen*. This atmosphere not only keeps the earth warm at night, but also protects it from dangerous radiations.

On the Surface

The earth's thin and cool crust has been broken up into many huge plates due to the movements in the hot and thick mantle. The boundaries of these plates are marked by earthquake zones dotted with volcanoes, and mountain ridges pushed up, where moving plates collide.

Quick Facts

- The crust of the Earth is a very small part of its vast mass.
- The heat that rises from the mantle pushes the plates of the crust apart.
- Mountains are formed whenever the oceanic crust is dragged beneath the continents.
- More than 70 percent of the earth's surface is made up of ocean water.

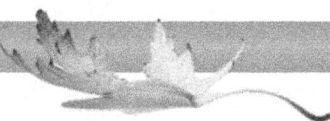

Chapter - 2

PLATE TECTONICS

The outer covering of the earth is a *brittle shell*, known as the **crust**. Below the crust is a deep layer of hot rock called the **mantle**. The heat produced within the earth makes the mantle move, but very slowly. This movement makes the crust crack and break up into separate plates, which are being pushed together in some places and pulled together in others. When the plates move, they carry the continents around the globe, and also make oceans smaller or larger.

Parts

There are about *40 small tectonic plates* and *15 large ones*. They form the ocean floors, and some of the largest even carry the *continents*. The rocks from which continental plates are made are thicker, but much lighter, than the rocks of the ocean floor. The continents continue to move, but unlike the oceanic parts of the plates, they do not usually change shape and size.

Plate Boundaries

The plate boundaries are at some places pushed together, while at others, they are pulled apart. It might even be possible sometimes

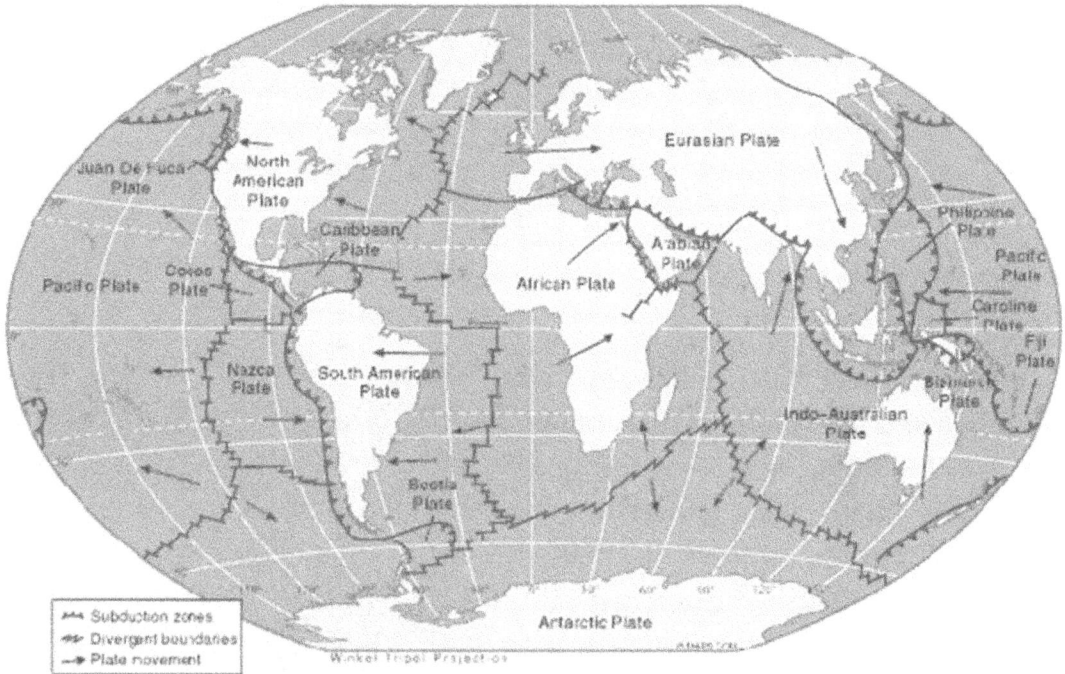

Subduction zones
Divergent boundaries
Plate movement

that one plate slides against another. Many plate boundaries are dotted with volcanoes, which may go off due to such movement. Earthquakes are also a result of these movements.

Convergent Boundaries

Convergent boundaries are found where a plate slides under another. For instance, ocean floors grind under continents. Due to this, mountain ranges are pushed up.

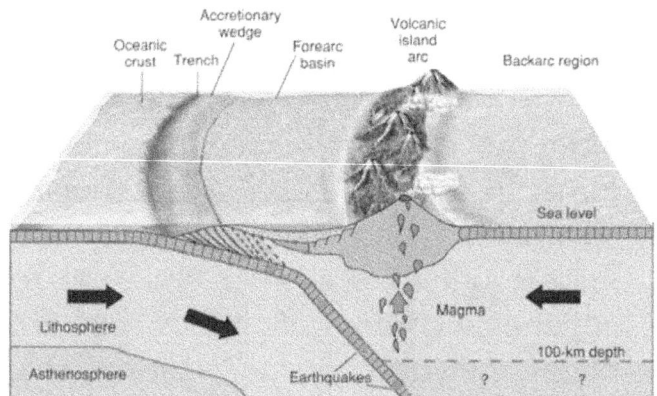

Divergent Boundaries

Divergent boundaries are formed where the plates pull apart. This usually occurs on the ocean floors. As the plates are pulled apart,

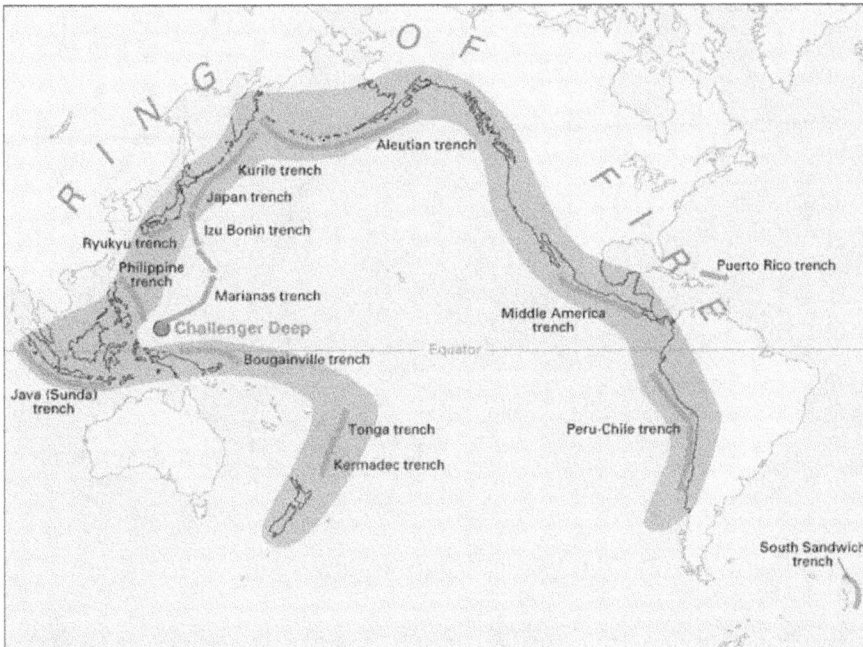

the hot mantle rock erupts in the rift zone and then solidifies as the new **ocean floor**.

Transform Boundaries

Transform boundaries are formed where two plates slide past each other. This causes frequent **earthquakes** along the *fault line* (a crack in the earth's surface usually caused by earthquakes).

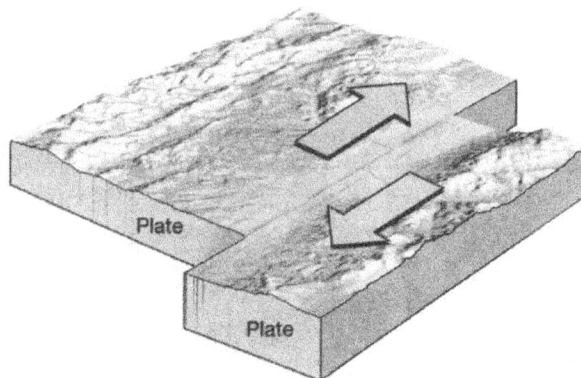

Globe

All the plates fit together perfectly to form the globe.

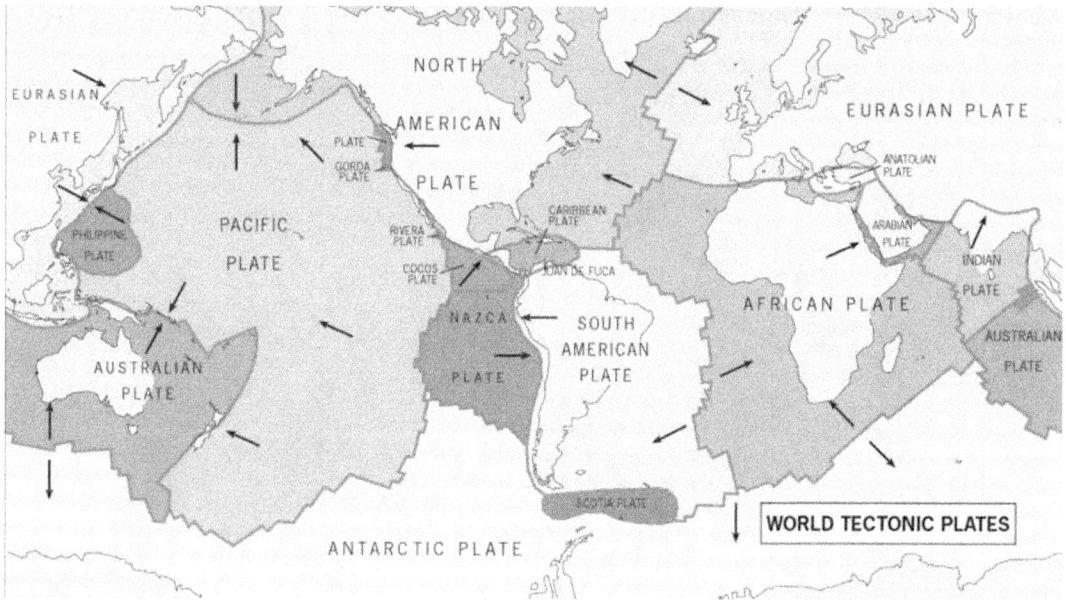

WORLD TECTONIC PLATES

Quick Facts

- Convergent tectonic plates move towards one another and the Divergent plates separate from each other.
- Transform plates slide together in a horizontal, vertical, or diagonal way.
- Every year, the seven continents move approximately 2 centimetres away from each other.
- Earthquakes are caused from transform plates.
- Some parts of the earth are either splitting or coming near each other.

Chapter - 3

EARTHQUAKES

The large plates of the earth's crust move continuously. Earthquakes take place when these plates meet and cause movement. Minor movement, that may even occur frequently, just causes **tremors** or shaking of the Earth, but what generally happens is that the rocks on the boundaries of each plate get locked together. The strain keeps on building up till the rocks get distorted and the locked section gives way. The rock then springs back, often shifting several metres, and the shock of this can cause a **disastrous earthquake**.

Earthquakes are recorded with the help of an instrument called the **seismograph**. It was devised by the **American scientist, Charles Richter in 1935**.

Chile, 1960

The biggest earthquake to be recorded in history struck **Chile** in **1960**. It reached *9.5 on the Richter Scale.*

Alaska, 1964

In this huge earthquake, within a span of a few minutes, the Pacific Ocean floor slid 20 metres (66 feet) beneath Alaska. Not too many lives were lost as very few people stay in this region.

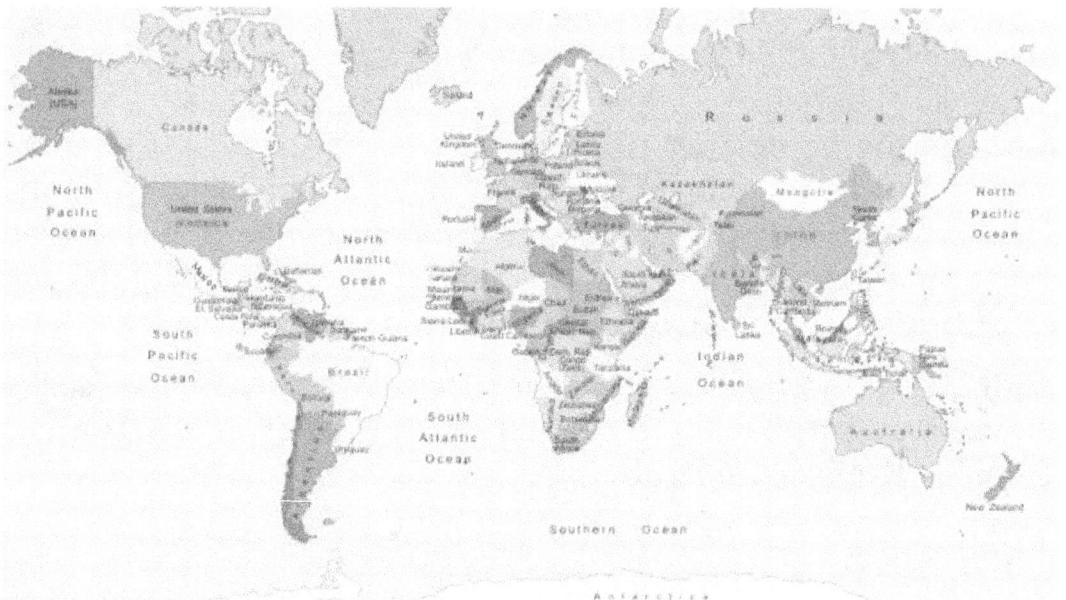

Mexico City, 1985

In 1985, a massive earthquake shook the city of Mexico. Over 400

multi-storeyed buildings were destroyed, and the death toll crossed 9,000.

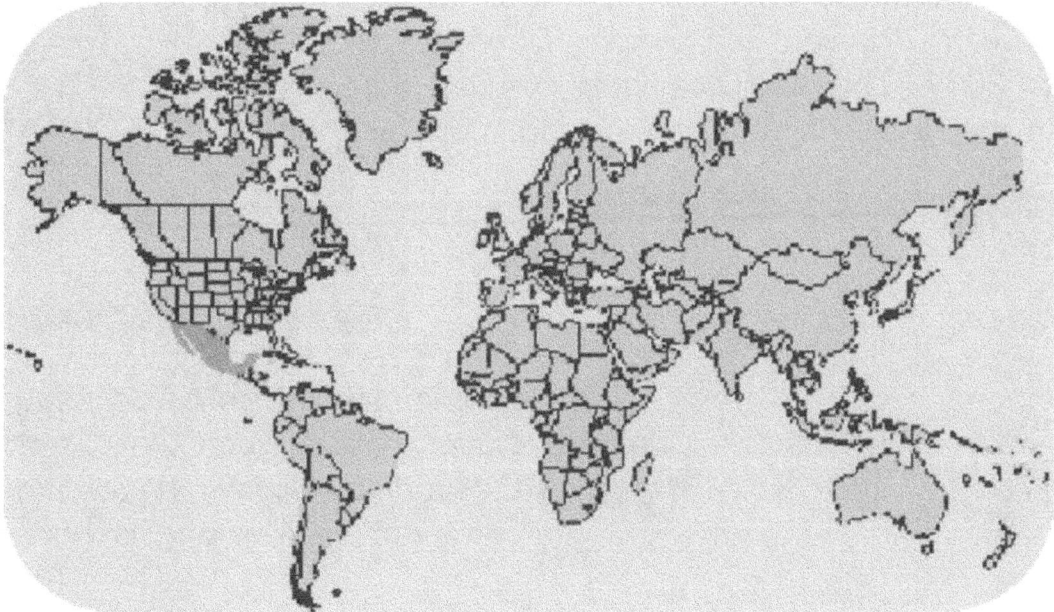

Kobe, 1995

Japan has more earthquakes than any other place on the earth. *Kobe, a city in Japan*, was severely damaged by a serious earthquake in 1995. It also resulted in the death of about 6,433 people.

Tsunami, 2004

An earthquake on the ocean floor off Sumatra caused the *Asian Tsunami in 2004*. This tragic calamity resulted in the death of more than 2, 83, 000

people. The shock caused huge waves which were sent across the *Indian Ocean*, devastating communities all around its shores.

Indonesia, 2006

A disastrous earthquake hit the island of **Java** in **2006**. It not only destroyed 1, 35, 000 houses, but also killed at least 5,780 people. A World Heritage site, the ancient **Hindu temple of Prambanan**, was also damaged but wasn't destroyed.

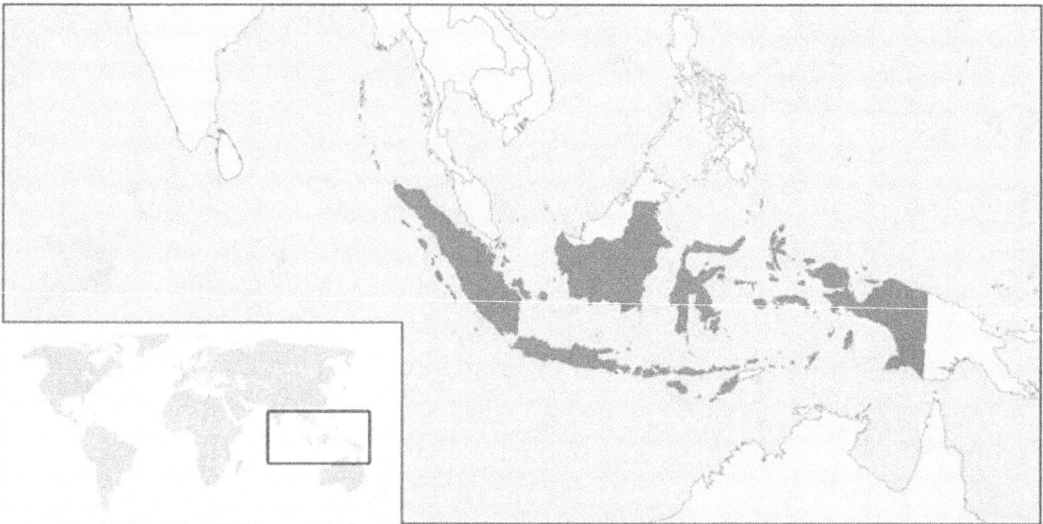

The Aftermath of the Earthquake in Indonesia, 2006

Quick Facts

- Earthquakes cause vibrations, and a seismograph machine records the motion of the ground during a quake. Scientists cannot predict a quake, but they can detect smaller regional vibrations along known as fault lines that may indicate that a bigger quake is coming.

- Since 1900, the largest measured earthquake on record was a magnitude of 9.5 in the Richter Scale in Chile on May 22, 1960. The second-largest was a magnitude of 9.2 in the Richter Scale in Alaska on March 28, 1964, the biggest ever in the United States.

- A tsunami is a sea wave caused by an underwater earthquake or landslide and a tidal wave is a large sea wave produced by high winds.

- It is estimated that there are about 500,000 detectable earthquakes in the world each year. About 100,000 can be felt by humans, and around 100 of them cause various degrees of damage.

- Sometimes, there are many small earthquakes before the big one. These small ones are called foreshocks. However, sometimes, after the big earthquake, the main shock, again there may be many small quakes. These are called the aftershocks.

- Many earthquakes happen on the ocean floor. Big ocean waves can form after a quake resulting in a tsunami.

- The shaking of the ground is not what kills most victims of earthquakes. The main killers in earthquakes are falling buildings, fires, landslides, avalanches and tsunamis.

- An earthquake happens somewhere in the world once every thirty seconds.

- You may not notice a magnitude 2 quake. You would feel the ground shake in a magnitude 3 quake. A magnitude 7 or higher can destroy a city.

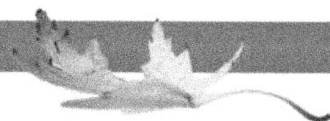

Chapter - 4

THE VOLCANOES

The word, *volcano* is derived from the name of Vulcano, a *volcanic island in the Aeolian Islands of Italy* whose name in turn originates from Vulcan, the name of a *God of fire in Roman mythology*.

Volcanoes are the most destructive of all the geological features of the earth. Generally, volcanoes are located along the boundaries of the plates, where the rocks that make up the crust of the earth meet. Friction of plates grinding against each other and opening rifts make the hot rock beneath the crust melt and burst up through **fissures** (cracks). Volcanoes may also occur over hotspots away from the plate boundaries, caused by the rising plumes of heat in the mantle beneath the earth's crust.

A volcano is basically an opening, or rupture, in a planet's surface or crust, which allows hot **magma**, **volcanic ash** and **gases** to escape from below the surface.

Ash **plumes** reach a height of about 19 km during a *volcanic eruption at Mount Pinatubo, Philippines in 1991*.

Erupting volcanoes can pose many hazards, mainly in the immediate vicinity of the eruption. Volcanic ash can be a threat to aircraft, particularly those with jet engines where ash particles can be melted by the high operating temperature. Large eruptions can affect temperature as ash and droplets of sulphuric acid obscure the sun and cool the **earth's lower atmosphere or troposphere**. However, they also absorb heat radiated up from the earth, thereby warming the *stratosphere*. Historically, the so-called *volcanic winters* have caused *catastrophic famines*.

Volcanoes are generally found where *tectonic plates are diverging or converging*. A mid-oceanic ridge, for example, the **Mid-Atlantic Ridge**, has examples of volcanoes caused by divergent tectonic plates pulling apart and the Pacific Ring of Fire has examples of volcanoes caused by convergent tectonic plates coming together. By contrast, volcanoes are usually not created where two tectonic plates slide past one another. Volcanoes can also form where there is stretching and thinning of the earth's crust in the interiors of plates, e.g., in the East African Rift, the Wells Gray-Clearwater Volcanic Field and the Rio Cleveland Volcano in the Aleutian Islands of Alaska and the Grande Rift in North America.

This type of volcanism falls under the umbrella of "Plate hypothesis" volcanism. Volcanism away from plate boundaries has also been explained as **mantle plumes**. These so-called 'hotspots', for example, Hawaii, are postulated

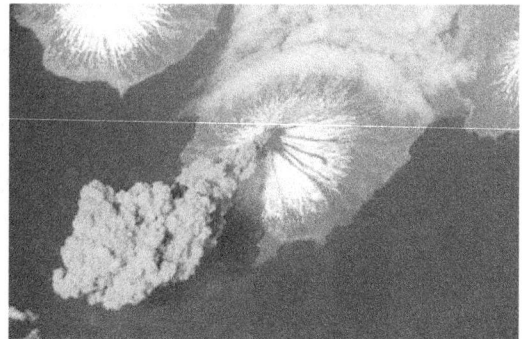

to arise from upwelling diapirs with magma from the core-mantle boundary, 3,000 km deep in the earth.

The study of volcanoes is called **Volcanology**, sometimes spelled **Vulcanology**.

Quick Facts

- The gas clouds that are a result of volcanic eruptions are mainly made of sulphur dioxide, water vapour and carbon dioxide.

- Lava bombs are cooled down forms of the molten rocks that erupts from volcanoes.

- Lava flows downhill at speeds of up to 100 kilometres per hour (60 miles per hour).

- The lava that erupts glows and is bright orange in colour because of its immensely high temperature of approximately 1,000°C (1,830°F).

- A hundred kilometres an hour is the approximate speed of the molten lava that flows downhill.

Chapter - 5

THE MOUNTAINS

When the plates of the earth's crust grind together, the edges of the continental plates are pushed up into *high, folded ridges*, called the *mountains*. When hot rock from beneath the surface erupts through the cracks in these mountains, *volcanoes* are formed.

Mount Everest

Lying around *8,850 metres (29,035 feet) above the sea level, Mount Everest* is the highest peak in the world. It is a part of the *Himalayan range*, which lies in India. These mountains were formed *50 million years ago*, when India collided with Asia. The Himalayas continue to rise as India is still moving towards the north.

Mount Aconcagua

Mount Aconcagua is the highest peak of the Andes mountain range,

which lies in South America. Its height is about 6,959 metres (22,834 feet). This mountain range is very prone to earthquakes.

Mount McKinley

The highest peak of North American Western Cordillera, Mount McKinley, is around 6,194 metres (20, 321 feet) above the sea level. It is located in Alaska, and due to its isolation is one of the most remarkable mountains of the world.

Mount Kilimanjaro

Mount Kilimanjaro is the highest peak in Africa. In reality, it is not a mountain, but a *huge volcano* with three volcanic cones. Out of the peaks of the three cones, the tallest is **Kibo**, which rises about 5,895 metres (19,340 feet) above the sea level. The other two cones are called *Shira and Mawenzi.*

Mauna Kea

The highest point on Hawaii is the top of a huge volcano that rises 10,000 metres (33,000 feet) from the Pacific Ocean floor. So although its peak is only 4,205 metres (13,796 feet) above the sea level, it is the biggest mountain on the earth.

Vinson Massif

Vinson Massif at about 4,897 metres (16, 067 feet), is the highest point of the Ellsworth range. It is located in Antarctica, which is a frozen continent.

Mont Blanc

The European Alps were formed due to the movement of the African continent towards the north. The highest peak of these European Alps is the Mont Blanc, which rises about 4,808 metres (15,774 feet) above the sea level. This height is not fixed and continues to change as its summit is a dome of ice.

Aoraki

Commonly known as *Mount Cook*, Aoraki is *New Zealand's highest peak*. Aoraki was 2,754 metres (12,317 feet) high, but after a landslide in 1991, its height was reduced by 10 m (33 ft).

Quick Facts

- More than 3,000 climbers have reached the summit of the Mount Everest.

- The snowy summit of Aconcagua is a part of the Earth's longest mountain range.

- Snow covers Mount McKinley all through the year.

- There is a 2.4-kilometre (1.5-mile) wide crater on Kibo's summit.

- The icy summit of Mont Blanc can rise to about 16 metres (52 feet) above its highest rocky peak.

Chapter - 6

THE OCEANS

More than *two-thirds of the earth's surface is covered with oceans.* The average depth of the oceans is 3.8 kilometres (2.4 miles). These oceans are not merely pools of salty water. The ocean floors are the areas where the great plates of the earth's crust split apart or grind together, creating long, high **ridges** and deep **trenches** dotted with *volcanoes.* As a result of this, the oceans change their shape and size all the time.

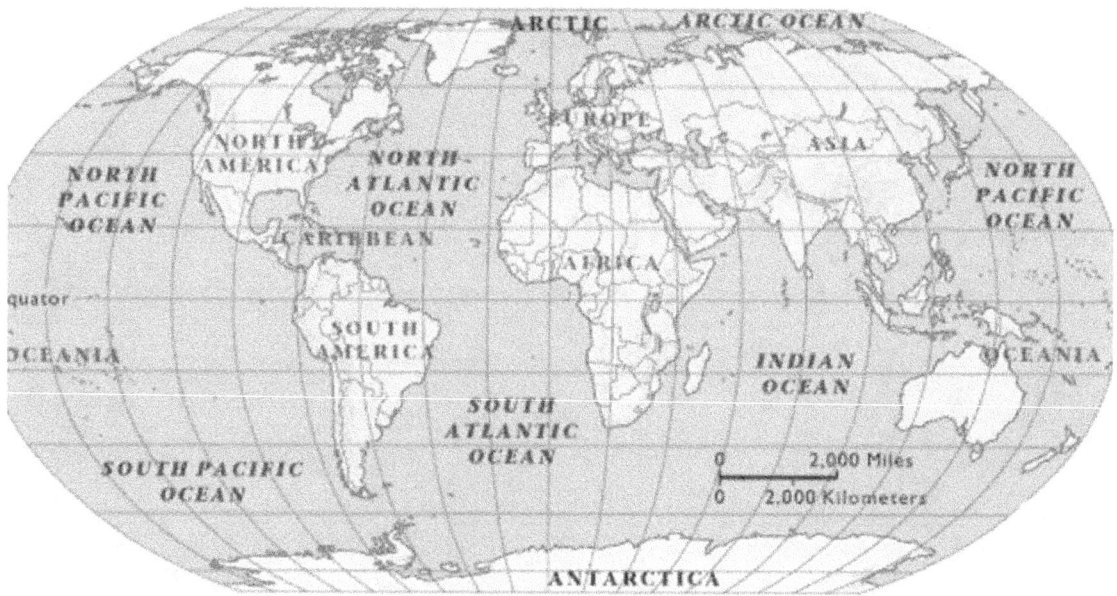

Major Oceans of the World

The Pacific Ocean

As big as all the oceans put together, the Pacific Ocean is now shrinking. The reason behind this is that the edges of its floor are slipping into deep ocean trenches (a hollow space created in the ground for laying pipes or getting rid of accumulated water), such as the **Mariana Trench**.

The Atlantic Ocean

When North and South Africa broke away from Europe and Africa and moved towards the West, the Atlantic Ocean was formed. The ocean continues to grow as a new ocean floor is created at the *Mid-Atlantic Ridge*. The ridge breaks the surface in the north to form *Iceland*, with its *volcanoes* and *geysers*.

The Arctic Ocean

Thick floating ice covers most of the Arctic Ocean. During spring, most of this ice melts, which allows the sunlight to reach the cold waters and helps the ocean life to grow and sustain itself. Though the sea near the North Pole stays

frozen even during the summer months, the area covered by ice is shrinking *every year* due to *global warming*.

The Indian Ocean

The Indian Ocean is basically a *tropical ocean*. It is very prone to *tsunamis*. It was last hit by a *tsunami in 2004*, which caused massive destruction on nearby coasts and various low-lying coral islands like the Maldives.

The Southern Ocean

The Southern Ocean is also called the *Antarctic Ocean*. With no obvious northern boundaries, the Southern Ocean forms a ring of cold, stormy water around Antarctica. Ice covers a large area in winter, and the giant icebergs that break off the Antarctic glaciers and ice shelves sometimes drift well towards the north.

- The oceans cover around 71% of the surface of the earth and contain about 97% of all the water on the planet.

- The Pacific Ocean is the largest water body on the earth, and takes up one-third of the planet's surface. The Pacific Ocean's name has an original meaning of 'peaceful sea'.

- Ocean tides are caused by the earths rotation, while the moon and the sun's gravitational pull acts on the ocean water.

- The average depth of the oceans is more than 2.5 miles.

- The Antarctic ice sheet that forms and melts over the ocean seach year is nearly twice the size of the United States.

- The world's oceans contain nearly 20 million tons of gold.

Chapter - 7

THE WEATHER

Without the various weather systems, continents would only be barren deserts. Life would not exist in such a place. However, weather can also be very violent and cause a lot of death and destruction.

Hailstones

Big *thunderclouds* have *upward currents*. These strong currents lift raindrops to a point, where the temperature is so low that they *freeze*. These ice pellets then fall down, but due to their light weight, are again carried upwards. As a result, more ice freezes on these *pellets*, turning it into a big hailstone.

Lightning

When ice crystals get tossed around in a cloud, they charge the cloud with a lot of *electricity*. This charge is then released as *a bright spark of lightning*.

Thunderstorms

The sun's heat makes the water from oceans, seas, rivers, lakes and ponds *evaporate* (evaporation is the process of vaporisation of liquid either naturally or by boiling) and rise in the air. Here the water cools down and starts to form clouds. Some clouds go as high as 15 kilometres (9 miles) or even more. These clouds contain a lot of water, which is eventually released as a dramatic thunderstorm.

Floods

Heavy rainfall generally causes the rivers to overflow their banks. This results in *flooding* of the surrounding areas, especially the low-lying areas of land. This river water may also rush down valleys, causing *flash floods* that destroy everything in their way.

Tornadoes

Rising moist, warm air forms *thunderclouds*. At times, this rising air develops into a tight, spinning *whirlpool of rising air*. This is known as a tornado. The speed of the wind inside the tornado can be more than 500 kilometres/hour (310 miles/hour), which can cause a lot of destruction.

Hurricanes

Hurricanes are *enormous storm clouds* that revolve around zones that have extremely low air pressure. They generally occur over the tropical oceans due to intense heat in these areas. The winds in a hurricane move in a circular motion and can reach a speed of about 300 kilometres/hour (185 miles/hour). Hurricanes formed over the Pacific Ocean are known as *typhoons*.

Quick Facts

- The tornado is the most violent of all the earth's storms and the average lifespan of a tornado is less than 15 minutes.

- One lightning bolt has enough electricity to service around 200000 homes.

- The fastest speed by which a falling raindrop can hit you is 18 miles per hour.

- During a hurricane, 90 percent of the people die from drowning.

- The coldest temperature ever recorded was a negative 126.9 degrees Fahrenheit in Vostok Station, Antarctica.

- The typical lifetime of a small cloud is between 10 to 15 minutes.

Glossary

Asteroids: Small solar bodies that orbit around the sun

Astronomer: A scientist who studies the various bodies in the Universe

Axis: An imaginary line through the middle of anything

Coma: The head of the material which is formed when a comet passes closer to the sun than the orbit of Mars

Diameter: The length of a line that cuts across the centre of a circular object from one end to the other

Equator: An imaginary line that cuts through the centre of the earth

Erosion: The process of removal of the earth's topmost layer

Evaporation: The process of vaporisation of liquid, either naturally or by boiling

Fault line: A crack on the earth's surface usually caused by earthquakes

Galaxy: A very large group of stars which are held together by the force of gravity

Gravity: A force that causes objects to fall on the ground

Impact craters: Structures formed when a huge comet, asteroid or meteoroid crashes into a planet or a satellite

Meteors: Short-lived streaks of light of meteorites; also known as shooting stars

Meteorites: Rocky materials from space that survive in the earth's atmosphere and land surface

Meteoroids: Rocky materials from space that come close to the earth

Nebulae: Thick clouds of hydrogen gas in which stars are born

Nuclear reaction: The process of reacting various chemicals to produce nuclear energy

Nucleus: A lump of dirt and snow, which forms a nucleus; also known as dirty snowballs

Oort cloud: A vast sphere formed by all the comets together

Seismograph: An instrument that records earthquakes

Spacewalk: An astronaut's movement in the space outside the aircraft or the spacecraft

Star cluster: A group of stars that are close to each other in space

Stargazers: People who study stars as an astronomer

Telescope: An instrument with lenses in it that help make distant objects look nearer

Trench: A hollow space created in the ground for laying pipes or getting rid of accumulated water

Typhoons: Hurricanes formed over the Pacific Ocean

Weathering: Breakdown of rocks, minerals and soils as a result of contact with the earth's atmosphere

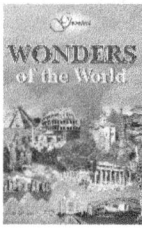

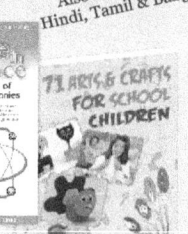

www.ingramcontent.com/pod-product-compliance
Lightning Source LLC
LaVergne TN
LVHW061221060426
835508LV00014B/1394